Plants and Animals
of Mount Rainier
and the Cascades

by Joe Dreimiller

Illustrated by:
Laura Fisher Romanelli
Sandy Harley
Dave Larson

ELTON-WOLF PUBLISHING

Design by Susan Picatti
Cover illustration by Laura Fisher Romanelli
Illustrations by Laura Fisher Romanelli,
Sandy Harley, and Dave Larson

05 06 07 08   5 4 3 2

ISBN: 1-58619-000-8
Library of Congress Catalog Card Number: 99-65652

Second Printing January 2005
Printed in Korea

Published by Elton-Wolf Publishing
Seattle, Washington

ELTON-WOLF PUBLISHING

2505 Second Avenue Suite 515   Seattle, Washington 98121
Tel 206.748.0345 Fax 206.748.0343
www.elton-wolf.com info@elton-wolf.com

TABLE OF CONTENTS

CREDITS / DEDICATION

A few individuals were of great help to us during the research process of this book. A special thanks to: Mary Henterly, Gina Rochefort, Ron Warfield, Rich Lechleitner and Lynn Allen.

Also, a special thanks goes to my wife Sharon, for her patience and support.

The National Association for Interpretation (NAI) was formed in 1988 from two existing organizations – the Association of Interpretive Naturalists and the Western Interpreters' Association. Both groups were created to provide training and networking opportunities for interpreters of natural and cultural history in non-formal settings.

This book was a NAI 2000 Book Award winner.

Dedicated to

Joseph Denn Dreimiller
Frank J. Pankiewicz
Two fathers who died early in their lives,
but inspired their families to explore
the natural wonders of the earth.

This guide was created to give a realistic image of the plants and animals found at Mount Rainier National Park and the Cascades. It was designed to be light-weight and to fit easily into one's pocket. I was a ranger at Mount Rainier between 1988 – 1995, spending most of my time in the subalpine meadows. I've met thousands of visitors on the trail wanting to know the names of certain plants and animals. I created this book with these people in mind.

I selected the most common plants and animals found in the Park and the Cascades and had them illustrated in color. Each diagram has a set of simple field marks for easy identification.

Something interesting about each animal and plant has been included to make the book a learning experience for all ages.

— Joe Dreimiller

HIKING TIPS

The following are some useful hiking tips that can make your visit to Mount Rainier and the Cascades more enjoyable.

• Most areas above 6000' usually have snow patches into late August. Hiking boots are the best, but if you're wearing sneakers take your time and stick your heels in the snow when coming downhill.

• If you're out hiking at higher elevations or on snow, please wear sunglasses to protect your eyes.

• Bring water for all hikes. Most people who visit the Cascades live at sea level. Your body will feel the effects of the higher altitude. Drink lots of water.

• Wear sunscreen. At higher elevations there is a greater concentration of UV light, and you will burn quickly. Remember, also, that the sun can reflect off the snow and burn you from beneath.

• Get a free map of the trails from a Ranger Information desk. The map that you get at the entrance is an overview of the Park and is mostly for cars. Each area of the Park has a simple hiking trail map.

• Stay off glaciers. All glaciers have crevasses which can be deadly if you fall in one. Most crevasses are over 100' deep. Stay on all trails to protect the meadows.

• All plants and animals are protected in the Park. Do not pick flowers or feed the wildlife. Most animals in the Park store food by producing fat. Human foods don't provide the nutrients needed for an animal to survive during the winter months (8). Most hibernators which are fed human food go to sleep and never wake up.

Amphibians are animals that live partly in water and partly on land. There are over 2500 species of frogs and 450 species of salamanders in the world. Mount Rainier has only 13 species. They are listed below:

Western Toad
Pacific Tree Frog
Tailed Frog
Red-legged Frog
Cascade Frog
Rough-skinned Newt
Ensatina

Northwestern Salamander
Long-toed Salamander
Pacific Giant Salamander
Van Dyke's Salamander
Western Red-backed Salamander
Larch Mountain Salamander

Amphibians develop through a process called metamorphosis, meaning their bodies change shape as they grow. For example, an adult frog will lay eggs in a pond. Tadpoles will hatch from the eggs, and they will have gills with which to breathe. As they grow bigger, the tadpoles will grow legs, their tails will disappear and they will develop lungs. The lungs will allow the young frogs to leave the water and travel on land. Some salamanders don't have a larval stage, but instead hatch as miniature adults.

Amphibian Characteristics:

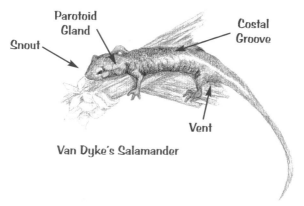

Van Dyke's Salamander

CASCADE FROG

(Rana cascadae)

Field Marks:
* Brown to olive above
* Black spots above
* Yellow jawline
* Toes slightly webbed
* Yellow belly

Notes:
* Lives near water
* Diurnal
* Frogs will swim across the water to escape predators rather than dive below the surface.

RED-LEGGED FROG

(Rana aurora)

Field Marks:
* Red behind legs and on belly
* Red brown to gray above with black flecks and blotches
* Light jaw stripe
* Yellow groin patch

(Hyla regilla)

Field Marks:
- Black eye stripe
- Skin rough
- Color is green,
  tan or brown
  and can change
- Suction pads on toes

Notes:
- Hyla means of forest.
- Regilla means queenlet.
- Eats live insects
- Only male sings

Life cycle = eggs - tadpoles - adults (takes 2 months)

(Bufo boreas)

Field Marks:
- Green to gray with
  many dark blotches of
  reddish brown warts
- Thin light line down
  middle of back
- Oval parotoid gland
  behind eye

Notes:
- Parotoid gland oozes a poison to deter predators
  from eating the toad.
- Eggs laid in 2 string like formations
- Tadpoles stay in maternal groups.
- Toads are land dwellers and eat insects and worms.

NORTHWESTERN SALAMANDER

(Ambystoma gracile)

Field Marks:
- Prominent costal grooves
- Smooth and moist brown skin
- Light brown parotoid gland
- Light brown along top of tail
- Up to $9\frac{3}{4}$" long
- Larvae found in ponds

LONG-TOED SALAMANDER

(Ambystoma macrodactylum)

Field Marks:
- Long 4th toe on hind foot
- Prominent 12-13 costal grooves
- Yellowish back stripe
- Blunt head
- Body speckled with white, blue or silver spots
- Brown, black or grayish skin
- Up to $6\frac{1}{2}$" long

Notes:
- Usually found in alpine lakes
- Takes 2 summers for larvae to mature into adults
- Can breed when ice is still on the pond

(Dicamptodon tenebrosus)

Field Marks:
* Belly light brown
* Bulky body
* Skin brown to a reddish tint
* Brown marbled pattern on back
* Up to 13" long

Notes:
* Found in streams or mountain ponds
* Dicamptodon means twice-curved teeth.
* They bite.
* They are vocal with a yelp-like sound.
* Females can lay approximately 85 eggs which they will protect from predators. Larvae are brown with gills.
* They eat insects, slugs, snails, worms, frogs, other salamanders and mice.

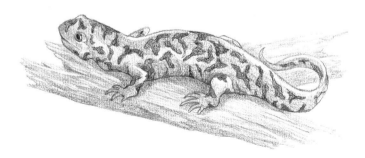

VAN Dyke's SALAMANDER

(Plethodon vandykei)

Field Marks:
* Two body colorations – reddish or dark brown sides with white spots and a yellow tail and throat
* 14 costal grooves
* Toes are partially webbed.
* Has a parotoid gland
* 4" long

Notes:
* Eggs laid on land and miniature adults will hatch from eggs
* Very rare species, only found in Washington State and only found in the Carbon River area at Mount Rainier

LARCH MOUNTAIN SALAMANDER

(Plethodon larselli)

Field Marks
* Brown to reddish back stripe
* Sides are grayish or black with white flecks.
* Belly is salmon colored
* 4" long
* Found only in lower forests

*Lungless salamander
(breathes through skin)

(Ensatina eschscholtzii)

Field Marks:
- 12 costal grooves
- Base of legs a yellowish to orange color
- Brown skin
- Orange belly
- 5" long

Notes:
- Can drop its tail to distract predators and grow a new one
- Secretes a milky poison to scare off predators
- No larval stage
- Eggs are laid and hatched underground.
- Found below 4500' in elevation

WESTERN RED-BACKED SALAMANDER

(Plethodon vehiculum)

Field Marks:
- 16 costal grooves
- Black sides
- Reddish brown to orange back
- 5" long

Notes:
- Eggs laid on ground and hatch as miniature adults
- Lives in moss and under logs
- Lives on land (terrestrial)
- Lungless

ROUGH-SKINNED NEWT

(Taricha granulosa)

Field Marks:
* Dry, rough skin
* Two variations of black, brown and olive green on back
* Orange belly
* No costal grooves
* 7" long

Notes:
* Found in lower forest to subalpine

It is poisonous and can secrete a poison that will kill most small mammals that try to eat it. The garter snake is not effected by the poison and can eat the newt. If you should handle this amphibian, please wash your hands afterwards as a precaution.

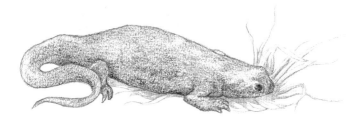

A reptile is an animal with a backbone (vertebrate) and scaly skin. There are 6000 types of reptiles in the world but only 6 species are found in the Park.

The characteristics of a reptile are a tough skin, waterproof scales and the laying of cleidoic eggs. Their eggs have a strong membrane which prevents them from drying out. A miniature adult will hatch from each egg. Some reptiles can bear live young, too. Since reptiles are cold-blooded, meaning their body temperatures are regulated by the weather, most need to warm up their bodies before they become active. This is why you see them basking on rocks or dark surfaces. The rocks are their heating pads. The Mount Rainier species are:

Northern Alligator Lizard
Western Skink
Rubber Boa
Common Garter Snake
Northwestern Garter Snake
Western Terrestrial Garter Snake

WESTERN SKINK

(Eumeces skiltonianus)

Field Marks:
- Body dark brown to black
- Cream and brown striped
- Juveniles have bluish tint on tail.
- Adults have indistinct tail stripes.
- Have eyelids
- Breeding males will have orange on sides of head and tip of tail.

Notes:
- Nests under rocks
- Female lays 2-6 eggs
- Eats insects, spiders, earthworms and their brood
- Winter hibernation in the soil

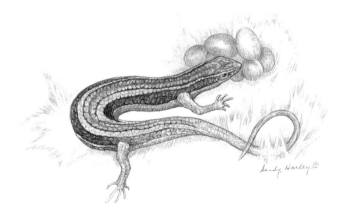

(Thamnophis ordinoides)

Field Marks:
- Yellow belly
- Green, brown, blue or black above
- Orange, red, black or yellow stripes
- 7 upper lip scales
- Scales keeled in 17 rows

Notes:
- Diurnal
- Mates twice a year, in the spring and fall
- 3-15 young are born alive
- Eats frogs, insects, salamanders, slugs and worms

Other snakes are:
Common Garter Snake - black with golden stripe on back/ red to black head/ reddish side spots (three subspecies)

Western Terrestrial Garter Snake - gray to black above/yellow stripes (two subspecies)

Rubber Boa - brown above/yellow beneath

A bird is an animal with feathers. They lay eggs and have specially adapted beaks instead of teeth. All birds have hollow bones and feathers, most have four toes for perching and build a nest for their young.

Nests can come in a variety of sizes, from a small depression in the ground, to eight feet across for an eagle. They are made of sticks, moss, leaves, lichens, grasses, lint and spider silk, depending on the bird species. Each type of bird also has a different diet. By observing the bird's beak (next page) you can usually identify its main food source.

There are over 8600 species of birds in the world. Mount Rainier has 163 species that appear annually. Only 88 of the species nest in the Park. Ornithologists, people who study birds, haven't done a complete Park study since the 1970s. If you are hiking and observe a rare bird, please fill out an Observation Card at a Ranger Information desk so the information can be passed on to the Park biologists.

The diagram above the bird beaks is a quick reference to the bird's anatomy which will help you with identification. All animals have characteristics that help us identify them called Field Marks. This might be their color, beak type, flight pattern or their size.

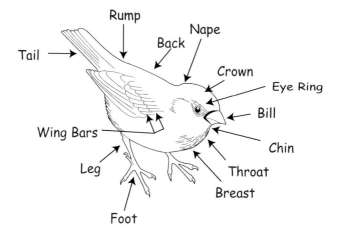

The shape of the bird's beak indicates
what the bird eats.

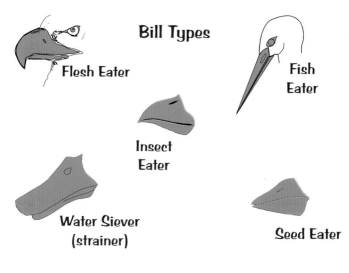

Bill Types

Flesh Eater

Fish Eater

Insect Eater

Water Siever (strainer)

Seed Eater

BIRD LIST

C = Common bird
U = Uncommon bird
   (seldom observed)
N = Nests in Park

Common Loon (U)
Western Grebe (U)
Great Blue Heron (U)
Canada Goose (U)
Green-winged Teal (U)
Mallard (U)
Northern Pintail (U)
Harlequin Duck (U, N)
Barrow's Goldeneye (U, N)
Common Merganser (U, N)
Osprey (U)
Bald Eagle (U)
Northern Harrier (C)
Sharp-shinned Hawk (U)
Cooper's Hawk (U)
Northern Goshawk (U, N)
Swainson's Hawk (U)
Red-tailed Hawk (C, N)
Rough-legged Hawk (U)
Golden Eagle (U, N)
American Kestrel (U)
Merlin (U)
Peregrine Falcon (U)
Prairie Falcon (U)
Blue Grouse (C, N)
Ruffed Grouse (U, N)
White-tailed Ptarmigan (U, N)
Killdeer (U)

Greater Yellowlegs (U)
Solitary Sandpiper (U)
Spotted Sandpiper (U, N)
California Gull (U)
Band-tailed Pigeon (U, N)
Western Screech Owl (U, N)
Great Horned Owl (U, N)
Northern Pygmy Owl (U, N)
Spotted Owl (U, N)
Barred Owl (U, N)
Northern Saw-whet Owl (U, N)
Common Nighthawk (U)
Black Swift (U)
Vaux's Swift (C, N)
Calliope Hummingbird (U, N)
Rufous Hummingbird (C, N)
Belted Kingfisher (U, N)
Lewis Woodpecker (U, N)
Red-breasted Sapsucker (U, N)
Downy Woodpecker (U, N)
Hairy Woodpecker (C, N)
Three-toed Woodpecker (U, N)
Black-backed Woodpecker (U, N)
Red-shafted Flicker (C, N)
Pileated Woodpecker (U, N)
Olive-sided Flycatcher (U, N)
Western Wood-Pewee (U, N)
Willow Flycatcher (U, N)
Hammond's Flycatcher (U, N)
Dusky Flycatcher (U, N)
Pacific-slope Flycatcher (C, N)
Horned Lark (U, N)
Tree Swallow (U, N)

Violet-green Swallow (C, N)
Barn Swallow (C, N)
Gray Jay (C, N)
Steller's Jay (C, N)
Clark's Nutcracker (C, N)
American Crow (U)
Common Raven (C, N)
Black-capped Chickadee (U)
Mountain Chickadee (C, N)
Chestnut-backed Chickadee
   (C, N)
Red-breasted Nuthatch (C, N)
Brown Creeper (C, N)
Winter Wren (C, N)
American Dipper (U, N)
Golden-crowned Kinglet (C, N)
Ruby-crowned Kinglet (C)
Western Bluebird (U)
Mountain Bluebird (U, N)
Townsend's Solitaire (U, N)
Swainson's Thrush (C, N)
Hermit Thrush (C, N)
American Robin (C, N)
Varied Thrush (C, N)
American Pipit (C, N)
Cedar Waxwing (U, N)
European Starling (U, N)
Solitary Vireo (U, N)
Warbling Vireo (U, N)
Orange-crowned Warbler (U, N)
Nashville Warbler (U)
Yellow Warbler (U, N)
Yellow-rumped Warbler (C, N)

Black-throated Gray Warbler (U)
Townsend's Warbler (C, N)
Hermit Warbler (U, N)
McGillivray's Warbler (U, N)
Common Yellow-Throat (U, N)
Wilson's Warbler (C, N)
Western Tanager (U, N)
Black-headed Grosbeak (U, N)
Chipping Sparrow (U, N)
Savannah Sparrow (U, N)
Fox Sparrow (U, N)
Song Sparrow (U, N)
Lincoln's Sparrow (U, N)
White-crowned Sparrow (C, N)
Golden-crowned Sparrow (U)
Dark-eyed Junco (C, N)
Red-winged Blackbird (U, N)
Brewer's Blackbird (U)
Brown-headed Cowbird (U, N)
Gray-crowned Rosy Finch (U, N)
Pine Grosbeak (U, N)
Purple Finch (U, N)
Cassin's Finch (U, N)
Red Crossbill (U, N)
White-winged Crossbill (U)
Pine Siskin (C, N)
American Goldfinch (U)
Evening Grosbeak (U, N)
House Sparrow (U, N)
Rufous-sided Towhee (U)

Pied-billed Grebe
Wood Duck
Blue-winged Teal
Cinnamon Teal
American Wigeon
Ring-necked Duck
White-winged Scoter
Bufflehead
Hooded Merganser
Turkey Vulture
Ferruginous Hawk
California Quail
Virginia Rail
Semipalmated Sandpiper
Baird's Sandpiper
Common Snipe
Wilson's Phalarope
Red-necked Phalarope
Ring-billed Gull
Caspian Tern
Marbled Murrelet

Mourning Dove
Williamson's Sapsucker
Northern Rough-winged
    Swallow
White-breasted Nuthatch
Barn Owl
Snowy Owl
Long-eared Owl
Boreal Owl
Black-billed Magpie
Bushtit
Pygmy Nuthatch
Canyon Wren
Northern Shrike
Lazuli Bunting
Vesper Sparrow
Snow Bunting
Western Meadowlark
Common Redpoll

(Junco hyemalis)

Field Marks:
* Gray to brown coloration
* Whitish belly
* Pinkish bill
* Dark head
* In flight, sides of tail are white and middle of tail is dark gray

Notes:
* Hyemalis means of winter
* Ground nester

In winter, Juncos eat mainly seeds, but on warm winter days they will eat insects off the top of the snow which are wind traveled. In summer, they eat mainly insects and berries.

The Oregon Junco and White-winged Junco are now all clumped under one name; the Dark-eyed Junco.

(Selasphorus rufus)

Field Marks:
- Male has a red throat and a rufous (red-brown) color on back.
- Female has a green back and rufous color at base of tail and on its sides.

Notes:
- Nests in salal, ferns and dead trees bearing lichen
- Nest made with lichens and spider silk
- Preferred food plants are wild currants, fireweed paintbrush, penstemon and salmon berry
- Male defends food sources within its territory.
- Migrates in winter to central Mexico

(Stellula calliope)

Field Marks:
*   Green head
*   Green back and tail
*   Males have reddish streaked throat

Notes:
*   Smallest bird in North America
*   Weighs $\frac{1}{10}$ of an ounce
*   Stellula means little star.
*   Breeds at higher elevations 4000-8000'
*   Nest made of bark, moss, lichen, pine needles and spider silk
*   Migrates in winter to central Mexico

GOLDEN CROWNED SPARROW

(Zonotrichia atricapilla)

Field Marks:
* Yellow crown bordered by black

Notes:
* Called the rain bird by some, its song precedes rain
* Eats insects and flower seeds

(Regulus calendula)

Field Marks:
- Greenish above
- A broken white eye ring
- Two white wing bars
- Black band below second wing bar
- Black bill
- Ruby crown only on males

Notes:
- Calendula means small glow.
- Eats insects mostly off tree bark and foliage
- Golden-crowned Kinglet (Regulus satrapa) is another Park bird. The male of this species has an orange crown and the female a yellow crown.

(Cyanocitta stelleri)

Field Marks:
- Black crested head
- Black shoulders and breast
- Lower half of bird is ultramarine blue

Notes:
- Named after George Steller, a naturalist and explorer
- Builds nest made of twigs and dead leaves
- Eats mainly seeds and berries, but has been known to eat other birds' eggs, too

(Perisoreus canadensis)

Field Marks:
- Dark gray underparts and crown
- Whitish face and forehead
- Light gray on belly
- Young - dark slate colored
- Smaller than Clark's Nutcracker

Notes:
- Other names: Canada Jay, Camp Robber, Whiskey-Jack

Call: Whee-oh

It stores food for the winter by mixing seed bundles with their sticky saliva and leaving it in bark crevices.

CLARK'S NUTCRACKER

(Nucifraga columbiana)

Field Marks:
- Pale gray
- White streak on black tail and black wings
- Black bill

Notes:
- Nucifraga columbiana means nut break after the river.
- Member of the crow family

These birds store thousands of seeds in the fall for a winter supplemental food supply.

(Troglodytes troglodytes)

Field Marks:
* Tiny
* Short tail
* Dark brown upper parts
* Black bars on tail, wings and belly
* Light line over eye

Notes:
* Troglodytes means cave dweller. The bird likes dark, dense undergrowth.
* Eats insects
* Has one real and several decoy nests, all camouflaged

Call: high trills followed by shallow buzzes

Nest made of twigs with moss lining in rock crevices and nearly exposed tree roots

VARIED THRUSH

(Ixoreus naevius)

Field Marks:
- Males - eye stripe and wing markings rusty brown, black breast band
- Females - yellow eye stripe, pale brown body, grayish breast band

Notes:
- Young birds look like adult females. Colors help them blend with the forest.
- Varied Thrushes nest in young saplings.
- Nest materials are twigs, grasses and mosses
- The Varied Thrush is a ground feeder. It eats worms, insects, berries, snails and seeds.

Call: two second long whistle about every ten seconds, every whistle a different pitch

(Dryocopus pileatus)

Field Marks:
- Male - red stripe on neck
- Red crest on head
- White wing patches in flight
- Large bird 14-18" in height

Notes:
- Pileatus means tree sword.
- Pecks large oval holes for nesting cavities
- Eats mainly carpenter ants
- The tongue, which is barbed at its tip, is longer than its head.
- The beak grows continuously throughout its life.

RED-SHAFTED FLICKER

(Colaptes cafer)

Field Marks:
- White rump visible in flight
- Brown back
- Salmon-red color under wings and tail
- Black crescent on chest
- Male has a red mustache

Notes:
- Omnivore - eats ants, beetles, crickets, fruits and berries
- The Yellow Shafted Flicker is also found in the region, but has a yellowish color under its wings and tail.

(Dendragapus obscurus)

Field Marks:
- Yellow-orange patches on the neck
- Yellow-orange eyebrow comb
- Both sexes have a blackish tail.
- Males - mottled dark gray above and pale gray beneath
- Female - mottled brown and gray tipped tail

Notes:
- Other name is Sooty Grouse
- Obscurus means dark.

Its song is a low hooting sound. The male inflates air sacs in its throat to make the sound, which is used to attract a female.

NORTHERN HARRIER

(Circus cyaneus)

Field Marks:
- Long winged
- Long tail
- White rump patch seen in flight
- Male wings - gray above, white below, black wing tips
- Female wings - brown above, buff below
- Immature wings - brown above, cinnamon color below

Notes:
- Nest on ground
- Found in open meadows flying 10-20' off the ground while searching for rodents or small birds to eat

Formerly - Marsh Hawk

(Strix occidentalis)

Field Marks:
- Yellow bill
- White spotted chest
- White streaked below chest
- Dark eyes
- No ear tufts
- Wingspan to 42"

Notes:
- Found in old growth forests
- Nocturnal
- Protect their nest by dive bombing predators, including humans
- Acute hearing and sight
- Silent flight
- Small prey can be swallowed whole.

Sandy Harley

Mammals are characterized as animals that have hair and feed their young milk. Some common mammals are: opossums, whales, bats, primates, rodents, goats, shrews and cougars. Mammals are very diverse, with over 4000 species found worldwide. Mount Rainier has only 52 species, and most are rarely seen by visitors. Since 1934, several species have disappeared from the Park. The most recognized ones are the wolf, fisher, lynx, wolverine, muskrat and Pacific otter. Most of these species were trapped outside the Park for their valuable furs.

Mammals are adapted to eat different types of food during certain times of the day. The four main diets are:

1. Carnivore - meat eater
2. Herbivore - plant eater
3. Omnivore - meat and plant eater
4. Insectivore - insect eater

In the Cascades, most of the larger mammals feed during the day (diurnal) and the smaller animals at night (nocturnal).

We have selected 11 mammals which you are most likely to see, and they have been highlighted in the following list.

Big Brown Bat
Hoary Bat
Lump Nosed Bat
Hairy-winged Myotis
Little brown Myotis
Yuma Myotis
Silver-haired Bat

Dusky Shrew
Marsh Shrew
Masked Shrew
Trowbridge Shrew
Vagrant Shrew

Heather Vole
Oregon Vole
Water Vole
Townsend Vole
Pika
Coast Mole
Townsend Mole
Shrew Mole
Gapper Red-backed Mouse
Long-tailed Meadow Mouse
Pacific Jumping Mouse
White-footed Deer Mouse
Golden-mantled Ground Squirrel
Northern Flying Squirrel
Douglas Squirrel (Chickaree)
Townsend's Chipmunk
Yellow-pine Chipmunk

Northern Pocket Gopher
W. Bushy-tailed Woodrat

Coyote
Bobcat
Red Fox (black)

Short-tailed Weasel
Long-tailed Weasel
Pine Marten
Mink
Black Tailed Deer
Mule Deer
Elk

Mountain Goat
Snowshoe Hare

Beaver
Mountain Beaver
Spotted Skunk
Striped Skunk
Raccoon
Hoary Marmot
Porcupine

Mountain Lion
Black Bear

HOARY MARMOT

(Marmota caligata)

Field Marks:
- A large rodent
- Silvery/gray on back
- White stomach
- Black feet

Notes:
- Loud whistle-like sound for an early warning system
- Lives in colonies
- Diurnal
- True hibernator (6-7 months a year)
- Found in the meadows resting on a rock or munching flowers to gain fat for its winter sleep

(Martes americana)

Field Marks:
- Throat patch white, yellowish or orange
- Rich dark brown fur

Notes:
- Home range 5-15 miles
- Does not hibernate
- Prefers fir, spruce and hemlock forests
- Eats rodents, birds' eggs, berries, conifer seeds, carrion and squirrels
- 85% of their lives are spent in trees
- Endangered species

(Ochotona princeps)

Field Marks:
- A small logomorph
- Small rounded ears, white-bordered
- No tail
- Soles of feet padded
- Makes a loud eek, eek sound

Notes:
- Other names: Cony, Little Chief Hare, Rock Rabbit
- Princeps means Mongolian Chief.
- Member of the rabbit family
- Found 3000-8000' in elevation

Pikas make large haystacks of plants under rocks for winter food. They are active all winter in the rocks under the snow.

(Eutamias townsendi)

Field Marks:
- Black and creamy to graying stripes
- Whitish stripe on face
- Yellowish to brown body

Notes:
- Eutamias - means true storer.
- True hibernator
- Diurnal
- Usually found in the lower forest

The other species in the Park is the Yellow Pine Chipmunk (Eutamias amoenus) which has distinct black and white stripes. It is more of a golden color and is found at higher elevations such as Paradise.

GOLDEN-MANTLED GROUND SQUIRREL

(Spermophilus lateralis)

Field Marks:
- Larger than a chipmunk
- No white stripes on face
- White stripe from shoulder to base of tail
- Yellowish to brown fur

Notes:
- Spermophilus means seed lover.
- True hibernator
- Found mostly on the east side of the Park

(Felis concolor)

Field Marks:
- Light brown fur
- Long, dark tipped tail
- Large mammal in cat family

Notes:
- Nocturnal, can travel 25 miles a night
- Carnivore
- Solitary except when caring for young
- Kills by biting neck of prey
- Kittens are spotted for 6 months after birth and stay with mom for 2 years.
- Other names: Cougar, Puma

MOUNTAIN GOAT

(Oreamnos americanus)

Field Marks:
- Large white to gray colored mammal
- Cloven hoofed
- Both sexes have horns

Notes:
- Eats grasses, lichens, moss, flowers
- Defend themselves with horns and hooves
- Females give birth to 1 kid in late spring.
- Found in large groups with both males and females
- Popular viewing areas:
    Mildred Point
    On cliffs across from Nisqually Vista Trail
    Sunrise Meadows
    Mount Fremont

(Cervus elaphus)

Field Marks:
- White rump
- Mostly brown fur
- Darker brown on shoulders and neck
- Males antlered
- Bugle sounding

Notes:
- Native Americans called the elk Wapiti meaning white rump.
- Cows and calves graze separately from the bull herd, except in winter.
- Bulls can run 35 mph.
- Males weigh on average 700 pounds, females 500 pounds.

The Sunrise area and Steven's Ridge are popular elk areas in the summer.

(Odocoileus hemionus)

Field Marks:
- Reddish-brown to brown fur in summer
- Grayish color in winter
- Rump and throat whitish
- Inside ears and interior of legs white
- Tail is white with a black tip

Notes:
- The other species in Park is the Black-tailed Deer (Odocoileus hemionus columbianus). It has an all black tail.
- Mule deer are named for their mule-like ears.
- Female deer (doe) gives birth to twin fawns with spots.
- The fawns usually stay with mom for 2 years.
- On males (bucks) the antlers will grow continuously for life. Antlers are made of solid bone and branch into two nearly equal branches. Mature antlers have 4-5 points.
- Mule deer have several scent glands on their bodies to mark territories, mark their trails, or to attract mates. Glands are located near ankle joints, on forehead, between toes and inside of hind legs.
- Main predators of deer are cougars, coyotes, bears and bobcats. They usually kill the fawns or sick deer.

(Vulpes vulpes)

Field Marks:
- Three variations:
  Black phase - almost completely black
  Silver phase - black with silver tipped tail
  Cross phase - reddish brown with dark colors
  across shoulders
- The red fox in the Park is mostly black with grayish fur mixed in.
- All have a white-tipped tail.

Notes:
- Omnivorous
- They enlarge a marmot hole or dig a hole in a secluded hillside for a den.

BLACK BEAR

(Ursus americanus)

Field Marks:
- Fur color – black, brown, cinnamon
- Short tail
- Flat footed
- No shoulder hump

Notes:
- Omnivore – eats carrion, insects, flesh, fish and plants
- Hibernates part of the winter
- Cubs are born in January and February.
- Cubs are nursed by the mother bear (sow) in den until spring.
- Commonly seen in subalpine meadows
- Males are solitary and are only with females for mating.

Please do not approach bears, especially cubs.
The sow will protect her young. If the adult bear does a series of false charges, you are too close and you need to move back or the bear may attack.

50

I have always enjoyed hiking in the lower forest at Mount Rainier amongst the giant Douglas Firs and Western Red Cedars. Here in the shadows of these great trees grow many wildflowers. Most of these wildflowers have adapted broad leaves to capture reflected sunlight and to collect rainwater, essential ingredients for survival. The lower forest, below 3500' in elevation, receives on average 78" of rain a year. Mount Rainier's old growth forests are places to avoid the crowds and enjoy some solitude with the 300-800 year old trees. I have selected 15 plants which are the most common and can be found along most Cascade roadways.

Vanilla Leaf
Foam Flower
Spring Beauty
Lily-of-the-Valley
Twin Flower
Trillium
Calypso Orchid
False Solomon Seal
Skunk Cabbage
Bunchberry
Pinesap
Western Coral Root
Mountain Ash
Huckleberry (also Subalpine)
Devil's Club

(Round Trip Mileage)

Southwest Side (Longmire area)
- Trail of Shadows - .75 mile
- Round Pass - 4 miles
- Carter Falls - 2.4 miles
- Longmire to Cougar Rock - 2 miles

South
- Box Canyon
- Box Canyon to Nickle Creek - 1 mile

Southeast (Ohanapecosh)
- Ohanapecosh Campground to Silver Falls - 3 miles
- Grove of the Patriarchs - 1.5 miles
- Three Lakes Trail - first mile only

Northwest Side (Carbon River)
- Carbon River area
- Mowich Lake area

PLANT VOCABULARY

Anther: the pollen bearing part of the stamen

Bract: a very small or modified leaf, usually growing at the base of a flower or flower cluster

Calyx: the outer circle of flower parts, made up of sepals, usually green

Corolla: the showy part of the flower composed of the petals

Disk: the round, button-like center (as in a daisy) made up of disk florets

Disk Florets: tiny, tube-like flowers that make up the disk

Filament: the anther-bearing stalk of the stamen

Head: compact stem of small, stemless flowers

Involucre: leafy growth composed of bracts encircling the head or cluster

Irregular: having petals of different sizes and shapes

Leaflets: leaf-like part of a compound leaf

Lobed: with deeply indented margins

Ovary: lower enlarged part of the pistil

Petal: several petals compose the corolla. usually the colorful part of the flower

Pistil: seed-bearing central part of the flower, composed of the stigma, style, and ovary

54

Raceme: an elongated flower cluster with stalked flowers arranged on a central stem

Rays: the strap-like florets encircling the disk flowers

Regular: having petals of about the same size and shape

Sepal: a small, modified leaf near the rim of the flower, an individual segment of the calyx, usually green, but sometimes white

Spadix: a club-shaped stalk on which are crowded tiny blossoms

Spathe: the hooded or leaflike sheath partly enfolding the spadix

Spike: a longish flower cluster, with stalkless or near-stalkless flowers arranged along the stem

Spur: a hollow, tubular projection of a flower

Stamen: the pollen-bearing part composed of the anther and filament

Stigma: the sticky part of the pistil which receives the pollen

Stipule: small, leaf-like growth at the base of a stem

Style: the neck of the pistil, between the stigma and the ovary

Whorled: three or more leaves radiating from a single point on a stem

VANILLA LEAF

(Achlys triphylla)

Field Marks:
- 3 single fan-like leaflets
- 1 spike with many white flowers

Notes:
- Other names: May-leaf, Sweet-after-Death, Deerfoot
- Achlys refers to mist (grows in dimly lit areas).
- Triphylla means three leafed.
- If the plant is dried, it will have a vanilla fragrance.

(Tiarella trifoliata)

Field Marks:

- Leaves hairy and toothed
- Leaves 3 lobed
- Sparse raceme with tiny white flowers usually in groups of 3
- Sepals ¼ to ½" long
- 8-16" in height

Notes:
- Other names: Coolwort and False Miterwort
- Tiarella means crownlet.
- Trifoliata refers to its 3 lobed leaf.
- Plant found up to 3500' in elevation

SPRING BEAUTY

(Claytonia lanceolata)

Field Marks:
* Single pair of opposite leaves
* 3-10 white to pink flowers
* Each flower: 2 cupped sepals
                  5 petals white to pink
                  5 stamens
* Height 2-6" tall

Notes:
* Lanceolata refers to its narrow leaves.
* Claytonia refers to naturalist John Clayton.
* Blooms April to June
* Can also be found in
  subalpine areas

(Maianthemum dilatatum)

Field Marks:
- 2-3 leaves each 1-3" in length
- Parallel veined leaves
- White flowers
- 4 sepals - single whorl
- 4 stamens
- Red berries

Notes:
- Other names: Beadruby, Deerberry, May Lily

TWIN FLOWER

(Linnaea borealis)

Field Marks:
* Opposite leathery leaves
* Flower stalk - reddish with 2-6 leaves on lower half
* Flowers 2 per stalk
* White to pink bell-shaped flowers
* Four stamens - 2 long & 2 short, pinkish in color
* Hairy within corolla

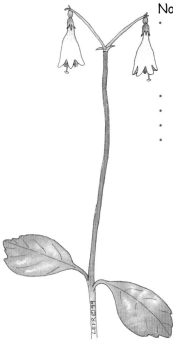

Notes:
* Linnaea refers to Carolus Linnaeus, 1707-1778, who developed the binomial system of naming organisms
* Borealis means northern.
* Honeysuckle family
* Very sweet fragrance
* It's a creeping evergreen which spreads over the ground by vine-like runners and by seed.

(Trillium ovatum)

Field Marks:
* 3 petals
* 3 sepals
* 3 leaves (3-7")
* 6 stamens
* Height 7-18" tall
* Flowers white and as it slowly ages, it will turn pink

Notes:
* Ovatum refers to leaf shape.
* Trillium blooms 2 years after germination.

(Calypso bulbosa)

Field Marks:
- Flower is slipper shaped
- Pinkish flower with white spots above and magenta streak beneath
- Nodding blossom

Notes:
- Other names: Fairy Slipper, Deers-head Orchid, Venus Slipper
- The Calypso Orchid needs a special fungus in the soil in order to grow.

- Found in late spring in the old Longmire Campground

(Smilacina racemosa)

Field Marks:
- Flowers white in one terminal inflorescence
- Leaves heavily veined, pointed and oval (2-7")
- Fruit is a green to red berry
- Height 2-3'

(Lysichitum americanum)

Field Notes:
- Early stage only spathe (large, 4 lobed yellowish bract) and spadix (fleshy flower stalk) are above ground. Leaves grow later.
- Flowers greenish yellow on 4-10" spadix
- 4 stamens
- Large 1-3' leaves

Notes:
- Pungent aroma attracts bees and flies for pollination
- Lily family
- Native Americans used the leaves to wrap their food for steam pit cooking.

The leaf stalks contain a chemical called calcium oxalate. It crystallizes into long barbed needles and needed to be boiled before the
Native Americans ate the plant.

(Cornus canadensis)

Field Marks:
- Leaf whorl of 6 green leaves
- 4 white leaf bracts (look like 4 large petals)
- In center of bracts are many white flowers each with: 4 sepals
  - 4 petals
  - 4 stamens
  - 1 pistil
- After flowering, red berries appear in a bunch.
- Height 2-8"

Notes:
- Other name: Dwarf Dogwood

Found in lower forest below 2500' and in shady areas

(Hypopitys monotropa)

Field Marks:

* Flowers are all on one side of stem
* Flowers turn down when young and up when mature.
* Unbranched stem
* Pale yellow plant
* Petals are fringed.
* Leaves scale-like
* 6-10 stamens
* Stigma extends beyond petals
* Height 4-12"

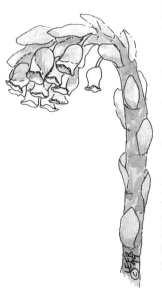

Notes:
* Hypopitys refers to under pines where it grows.
* Monotropa means turned one way.
* Other name: Many-flowered Indian Pipe
* Found usually as a single plant

It is a saprophyte which feeds on decaying plant material and does not have chlorophyll to photosynthesize (produce its own food).

(Corallorhiza mertensiana)

Field Marks:

- Lip reddish purple or white with 2 large purple blotches
- Wide spreading petals and sepals
- White, yellow, to red plant

Notes:
- Western Coral Root is a saprophyte. Before it can develop, it must be infected by a fungus. This is a symbiotic relationship where food and enzymes are shared.
- It has no roots or rhizomes.
- It takes several years before it can produce a seed stalk.

(Sorbus scopulina)

Field Marks:
- Two variations: a) var. scopulina - 13 leaflets
                   b) var. cascadensis - less than 11 leaflets
- Leaves pinnately compound
- Leaflets 1¼ to 2½" long
- Fine toothed at tip, not base
- Flowers white
- Red to orange berries

Notes:
- Found in dry rocky areas
- In the fall the leaves turn yellow or red.
- Also found in subalpine areas

(Vaccinium)

Field Marks:
- Blue, black and red berries
- Deciduous, alternate leaves
- Flowers white to pink and bell shaped
- 8-10 anthers
- Huckleberry plants 2-4' in height (bush)
- Blueberry plants 1-4' in height (bush)

Notes:
- Turns brilliant red in the fall on higher slopes
- Also found in subalpine meadows

(Oplopanax horridum)

Field Marks:
- Large maple like leaves, 7-9 lobed
- Leaves 6-15" in diameter and spines beneath
- Stalk densely spiked with spines
- Whitish spiked flowers
- Red berries (2-3 seeds per berry)
- Height 4-12'

Notes
- Oplo means weaponry.
- Panax refers to its large leaves.

Found in shaded,
moist areas

The subalpine meadows of Mount Rainier attract nearly two million visitors a year to view the magnificent floral displays. The subalpine flowers offer an array of color in yellows, blues, violets, oranges, reds, pinks, whites and purples. They all blend together with a majestic mountain sitting in the background. Due to the large amount of snow that falls in the Park, August is usually the best month to view the flowers. On average, the meadows receive 630" of snow a year.

As noted on the next page, many plants have adapted strategies for seed production and the attraction of pollinators. This enhances their chances of survival during the short growing season. Subalpine meadows are very fragile environments. Therefore, visitors should stay on the trail and should not pick the flowers.

POLLINATION AND PLANT ADAPTATION

Pollination is the process which most flowering plants use to produce seeds. Pollen is produced in the male plant parts called anthers. Each grain of pollen contains male sex cells. An insect will collect pollen and transfer it to the stigma, or the female part of another flower. When the pollen grain lands on the stigma, it will begin to grow downward into the ovule to fertilize the ovum. This begins the seed formation process.

The Cascades have several pollinators. The most common are:

- The Bumble Bees - which prefer yellow and blue flowers
- Flies - with 2 wings (Bees have 4 wings)
- Moths - which are attracted by scent and pollinate at night
- Butterflies - like red flowers
- Hummingbirds - prefer red flowers. The nectar is the hummers' sugary food source.

Plants in the Cascades need special adaptations to survive the harsh weather and short growing seasons. Plant adaptations are special characteristics a plant has to help it survive. Some examples of adaptations are:

- Pubescence - plant hairs which hold moisture and reflect UV rays
- Anthocyanin - a red pigmented chemical which helps warm the plant
- Pre-setting buds in the fall for next year
- Brightly colored petals to attract pollinators
- Having nectar guides to direct pollinator

Round Trip Mileage

Paradise Area
- Skyline Trail - 5 miles
- Lakes Trail - 5 miles
- Pinnacle Peak Trail - 3 miles
- Bench Lake/Snow Lake Trail - 2.5 miles
- Comet Falls Trail/Van Trump Park - 6 miles
- Nisqually Vista Trail - 1.2 miles
- Dead Horse Creek Trail - 2.5 miles

Longmire Area
- Eagle Peak Trail - 7 miles
- Indian Henry's - 11 miles from Kautz Creek
- Klapatche Park - 21 miles or 2 days

White River/Sunrise Area
- The Palisades - 7 miles
- Indian Bar - 14.5 miles (late summer trip)
- Summerland - 8.5 miles
- Sunrise Meadow Trails - .5 to 4 miles
- Naches Peak Loop Trail - 4.5 miles
- Tipsoo Lake - 1.2 miles
- Glacier Basin - 7 miles
- Grand Park - 13 miles

Carbon River Area
- Isput Creek Trail - 8 miles
- Tolmie Peak - 6.4 miles

Wonderland Trail - 93 miles around the whole mountain

(Senecio triangularis)

Field Marks:
- Arrowhead like leaves
- Leaves alternate on stem
- Leaves 8" long on bottom and are reduced to 3" near top
- Leaves sharply toothed

- Flowers yellow with 5-10 rays
- Multiple flowers on a single stem

Notes:
- Other name is Butterweed
- Senecio means old man.
- Triangularis refers to triangle shaped leaves.

Other Cascade species is Ragwort - Senecio Jacobaea L. It has spoon-like leaves with smooth edges.

(Arnica latifolia)

Field Marks:
- Leaves oval and opposite
- Height to 18"
- 8-15 yellow petals in a ray formation
- Petals ½ -1¼" long

Notes:
- Arnica means soft, like lambskin (leaf texture).
- Found in open areas

BUTTERCUP

(Ranunculus eschscholtzii)

Field Marks:
- Flowers yellow
- Waxy (cutaneous) sheen on their yellow petals
- 5 yellow smooth sepals
- Leaves long stemmed and 3 lobed
- Height 2-6"

Notes:
- 300 species worldwide
- Polymorphic perennial - many forms co-existing together
- Ranunculus means froglet.

(Potentilla flabellifolia)

Field Marks:
- Leaves like small fans
- 5 true sepals; between each true sepal is a bract, giving the appearance of 10 sepals.
- Notch-tipped petals
- 10 stamens
- 1" wide flowers
- Flowers yellow
- Height 5-10"
- Sometimes a pale-orange spot can be found at the base of each petal.

Notes:
- Flabellifolia refers to fan-like leaves.
- Three species found in the Pacific Northwest

GLACIER LILY

(Erythronium grandiflorum)

Field Marks:
- Broad elliptical leaves
- Golden yellow flower
- Anthers white, red, yellow or purple

Notes:
- Grandiflorum means large flowers.
- Large corm under plant is a popular bear food
- Found in drier sites like steep slopes and tops of hills
- One of the earliest flowers to emerge as snowpack melts

(*Gentiana calycosa*)

Field Marks:
* Leaves ovate
* Flowers deep blue
* 1 flower on each stem, sometimes 2
* Less than 12" tall

Notes:
* A deep-throated flower with the nectar and pollen at its base

When it begins to rain on the mountain it takes only seconds for the flower petals to close up. This mechanism ensures the pollen is protected from washing away. It takes the flower several hours to reopen.

Sections of the dark petals are transparent which allows light to pass through the petal structure. This provides light for the bees to see in order to access the nectar and to pollinate the flower.

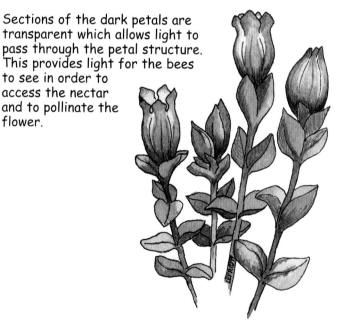

79

(Erigeron peregrinus)

Field Marks:
- Broad lance-like leaves
- Purple-blue flower
- Usually 1 flowerhead per stem
- At the base of the ray are 20-30 hairs.

Notes:
- Other name: Aster Fleabane

(Aster ledophyllus)

Field Marks:
- Alternate lance-like leaves
- Wooly gray beneath leaves
- Petals lavender to purple with 6-21 rays
- Many flowered heads per stem
- Cottony pubescence (plant hair)
- Height 12-25"

Notes:
- Another Cascade mountain
  species is Aster alpigenus.
  It has spoon shaped leaves and
  a single flower head
  per stem.

(Lupinus latifolius)

Field Marks
- Leaves palmately compound (like a palm)
- 7-9 leaflets 1¼" - 2⅜" long
- Hairy
- Flowers irregular
- Some of the lupine plants in the Cascades bloom in white.

Notes:
- Similar species: Alpine Lupine grows above 6000' (height 2"- 4")

- Only pollinated by bees
- The bee extends its head and mandible (mouth part) into lower part of upright petal and pushes against it to depress the keel (the two lateral petals). Pollen is then exposed and becomes attached to the underside of the bee.

(Penstemon procerus)

Field Marks:
- Lower leaves ovate, petioled, 4" long
- Upper leaves lance-like, 3" long
- Single stem
- Flowers blue to purple (Trumpet-like)
- Flowers two lipped whorled, ½" long
- Height 6-20"

(Veronica cusickii)

Field Marks:
- Leaves oval
- Four lobed corolla
- Pistil clubbed at top
- 2 stamens extending beyond petals

- Height 2-8"
- Large blue-violet flowers

Notes:
- Found above 5000'
- Plant stems are rhizomes.

Bouquets of this flower were given as a gift to someone taking a journey, thus the name Speedwell, from the saying "Go with God's speed."

(Dodecatheon jeffreyi)

Field Marks:
- 5 pink to purple reflexed (turned back) petals
- Enlarged stigma tip
- Leaves spoon shaped 2-16" long

Notes:
- Native American Legend - wherever a star falls to earth, these flowers appear
- Pollen is collected when bees vibrate the tip of the flower with quickened wing movements.
- Found in wet areas in the mountain meadows

L.E. FISHER © 97

MAGENTA PAINTBRUSH

(Castilleja parviflora var. oreopola)

Field Marks:
- 3-5 lobed leaves
- Magenta colored bracts, or flower parts
- Flowers are the green, tube-shaped feature within the bracts
- Corolla obscured by calyx
- Height 7-12"

Notes:
- Pollinated by hummingbirds

- There are many varieties of paintbrush in the Park, with shades of red, orange, yellow and white.
- Some common ones are: Obscure Indian Paintbrush, Scarlet Paintbrush, Small-flower Paintbrush and Cliff Paintbrush.

(Aquilegia formosa)

Field Marks:
- A nodding flower
- 5 red sepals as short straight reflexed spurs
- 5 petals
- Yellow center
- Petiole leaves in groups of 3

Notes:
- Formosa means beautiful.

LEWIS MONKEY FLOWER

(Mimulus lewisii)

Field Marks:
- Sticky, hairy stems
- Leaves opposite and attached directly to stem
- Leaves 2-3" long
- Petals deep pink
- Petals - lower 3 lobed and have a rose colored vein in the center
- Inside corolla is deep yellow and hairy
- Height 12-30" tall

Notes:
- Very common near streams

(Epilobium angustifolium)

Field Marks:
- Alternate Leaves
- 4-8" lance-like leaves
- Many pink flowers per stem
- Hairy near base of flower
- Height to 8'

Notes:
- It reproduces by seeds and rhizomes.
- The seeds are winged and easily dispersed by the wind.

WATERMELON ALGAE

Chlamydomonas nivalis

Notes:

In the late spring, red patches form on the snow
called Watermelon Algae. It smells like watermelon,
but don't taste it unless you want a mild digestive
problem. With the algae you might also find ice worms.
Ice worms (*Mesenchytraeus solifugus var. rainierensis*)
are small worms about 1" long. They collect nutrients
from the algae. Don't pick up the worm because it
needs a temperature of 32° to survive and the heat of
your hand will kill it.

(Phlox diffusa)

Field Marks:
- Leaves opposite and sharply pointed
- Flower has 5 petals
- Flowers can be pink, white, lavender and purple.
- 5 stamens

Notes:
- Diffusa means spreading.
- Plants need very little soil or water

Spreading Phlox is found on talus slopes or rocky areas where vegetation is blown. The vegetation and debris decay into soil.

The stamens, anthers and stigma are located at different levels on the inside of the flower to ensure that the insect pollinator's head will collect some pollen.

LEFR©99

(Spiraea densiflora)

Field Marks:
- Leaves oval 1½" long
- Leaves toothed
- Flowers rosy pink in dense, fuzzy, flat heads
- 25-50 stamens protruding from flower head
- Height 3-4' bush

Notes:
- Woody shrub
- Found 2000-11,000' in elevation
- Spiraea means wreath.

(Carex nigricans)

Field Marks:
- Leaves 4-9 per stalk
- Flower is a single black spike
- Stems of sedges have edges

Notes:
- Nigricans means blackish.
- Grass-like plant with a flower that has no petals
- Each flower stalk has male flowers (above) and female flowers (below).
- The plant is wind pollinated.
- Spreads by rhizomes
- 5-10 days after the snow melts away, it flowers.

SITKA VALERIAN

(Valeriana sitchensis)

Field Marks:
- 2 sets of opposite leaves
- Flowers lavender when young
- Flowers white when mature with lavender specks
- Height 12-48"

Notes:
- After the snow melts, deep reddish shoots of the new plant spring up.
- Like most plants in the sub-alpine meadows, the red in the plants is a chemical called anthocyanin. It helps the plant filter UV radiation, helps heat the plant and the new bud, and helps store carbohydrates in the roots. This is the same pigment that makes apples red.
- Fragrant smell

(Ligusticum grayi)

Field Marks:
- Flowers white in 1-3 inflorescences
- Basal leaves
- Stem to 24" tall
- 6 leaves compound (4-12" long) with parsley like leaves

Notes:
- Found in open and drier areas of meadows
- Other name: Gray's Lovage

BISTORT

(Polygonum bistortoides)

Field Marks:
- Leaves lance-like and jointed
- No petals
- Sepals 3-10 notched
- 8 stamens
- White flowers on a spike

Notes:
- Polygonum refers to its many jointed leaves.
- Bistortoides means twice crooked.
- Pungent smell which attracts flies for pollination
- Roots are thick and knotted.

The seeds germinate while attached to the parent stem. This accelerates the seeding process making the plant well adapted to the short growing season.

Other name: Dirty Sock Flower

(Anemone occidentalis)

Field Marks:
- Entire plant is hairy
- 5-7 white-purplish tinged sepals
- Flower white with 6 petals
- Yellow centers
- Leaves basal and divided
- Height of flower 4-6"
- After flowering, it will mature into a 12-24" soft feathery crown. ⟶

Notes:
- Anemone means wind.

Other names: Western Pasque Flower, Towhead, Windflower, Old Man of the Mountains

The plant is heliotropic which means it tracks the motion of the sun. The flower is always facing the sun maximizing the light it takes in. The light colored petals reflect the light into the center of the flower keeping it warmer than the outside air. This is an adaptation that attracts pollinating insects to the flower.

(Veratrum viride)

Field Marks:
- Leaves oval, pointed and parallel veined
- Looks like a corn stalk
- Flowers white to green
- Height 3-5' tall

Notes:
- Veratrum means black roots.
- Viride means green.

- Perennial herb
- All parts of plant are highly poisonous while the plant is in bloom. In the fall when the plant has gone to seed, the alkaloids go back to the roots and you'll see insects begin to eat the leaves.
- The plant doesn't need pigment in the flower to attract insects. It is pollinated by a nocturnal moth which is attracted by the plant's scent.
- The plant blooms every 5-7 years.

(Erythronium montanum)

Field Marks:
- 1 pair of broad lance-like leaves
- Petals white
- Yellow centers
- Anthers yellow
- Petals turn pinkish while drying out

Notes:
- Montanum means mountains.
- Found above 3500' in elevation
- The plant has the ability to bloom through the snow. It has anthocyanin which acts like antifreeze, preventing the plant from freezing. It is adapted to process newly melted snow. It pre-sets its bud to speed up plant growth and seed production. On sunny, days the flower faces out; on rainy days it will cup over, protecting its pollen.
- Reproduces by seed and runners
- It takes a plant 7 years to produce a flower, so a plant with 3 flowers may be 10 years old.

MARSH MARIGOLD

(Caltha biflora)

Field Marks:
* Leaves round
* White flowers in pairs

Notes:
* Buttercup family
* Insect pollinator
* A waxy coating over
  the petals and leaves
  prevents moisture loss
  during sunny days.

Found in very wet areas

PARTRIDGEFOOT

(Luetkea pectinata)

Field Marks:
* Leaves resemble birds' feet (tufts)
* Small white to cream flowers
* Height 4-6"
* Member of the rose family

Notes:
* Luetkea refers to Count
  Lutke, a Russian explorer,
  1797-1882.
* Pectinata means comb-like.
* Usually found where the
  snow melts last. The
  leaves can persist
  through winter.

(Xerophyllum tenax)

Field Marks:
- Basal leaves in a clump at base of plant
- Flower stalk 2-5' tall
- Hundreds of small white flowers on stalk
- 6 stamens per flower

Notes:
- Xero means dry.
- Phyllum means leaf – refers to dry and tough leaves.
- Blooms only once every 7-10 years, then plant dies
- Lily family
- Other Names: Indian Basket Grass, Squawgrass
- Flowerheads bloom from the bottom up. This way seed production is staggered.
- Mountain goats eat the mature leaves, while black bears eat the tender young leaves and root stalks.

(P. groenlandica)

Field Marks:
*   Flower pink and looks like an elephant's head.
*   Many flowers on a stem
*   Height 12-24"

Notes:
*   This flower is bee pollinated. The head contains

the nectar and the trunk the pollen. These flower parts are the same distance apart as the length of the bee. As the bee gets nectar, the pollen is attached to the bee's legs and abdomen. Then the bee will transport the pollen to another pedicularis.

(P. racemosa)

Field Marks:
- Leaves toothed and reddish (early)
- Flowers a pale pink
- Flower - beak curled sideways and downward
- Height 5-24"

Notes:
- Racemosa means bearing racemes.

RAINIER PEDICULARIS

(P. rainierensis)

Field Marks:
- Leaves on stem and at base
- Leaves fern-like, 6-16"
- Flowers yellow to cream
- Swirl pattern of yellow flowers near top of stalk
- Long tube flowers ending in a narrow hook on a small lip

Notes:
- Mt. Rainier is the only place in the world where this plant grows.

(P. bracteosa)

Field Marks:
- Alternate leaves top part of stem
- Leaf attached to stem
- Purple leaves on plants near end of growing season
- Flowers yellow to pink
- Many flowers on spike
- Flower barely beaked
- Height 2-3'

Notes:
- Early bloomer

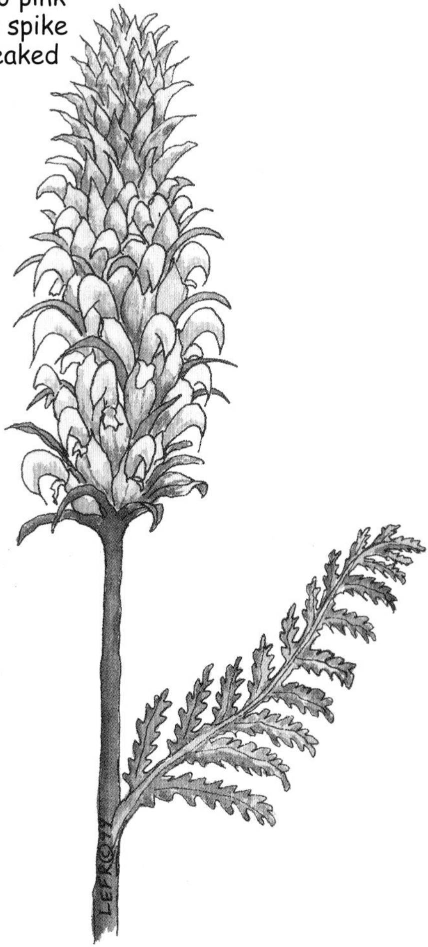

(P. contorta)

Field Marks:
- Fern-like leaves at base
- Flowers pale yellow to white
- Beak semicircular and arched back towards lower lip like a shepherd's crook
- Height 6-24"

Notes:
- Grows in dry raised areas

(P. ornithorhynacha)

Field Marks:
- Leaves green above and purplish below
- Flowers pinkish
- A thin down-turned beak that is straight

Notes:
- May be found on dry pumice at higher elevations

HEATHERS

The three heathers in this section are not true heathers, but a Moss Heath. However, they are commonly referred to as heather. These flowers are deciduous. After pollination the bells will fall to the ground. On true heathers the bells will remain on the stems, turn brown and the seed will ripen within the capsules. Heather grows approximately 1" a year and is considered a very fragile plant in the meadows. A human foot-print on heather can slow its growth by years. Both genera are named for Greek mythology characters. Phyllodoce means sea nymph, and Cassiope is the wife of King Cephus of the Ethiopians.

WHITE HEATHER

(Cassiope mertensiana)

Field Marks:
* Corolla bell shaped and white
* Leaves scale-like
* Leaves in rows of 4, flattened and overlapping (imbricated) to the stem
* Stems dark green
* Height 2-12"

Notes:
* Some plants near Panorama Point on the Paradise side are over 10,000 years old.

(Phyllodoce empetriformis)

Field Marks:
- Leaves needle-like (evergreen)
- Brownish stems
- Corolla bell shaped and pink
- 5-15 flowers per stem
- Height 4-15"

Notes:
- Stem diameter of a pencil can represent 50 years of growth
- It has a waxy cuticle on its leaves to prevent water loss.
- The meadow vole is the heather's natural pruner. It tunnels underneath the winter snowpack and eats the heather leaves. This munching also produces debris which over time becomes soil.

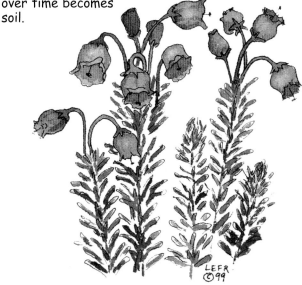

YELLOW HEATHER

(Phyllodoce glanduliflora)

Field Marks:
- Leaves needle-like, ¼" long
- Leaves spread out at right angles to the stem
- Yellow corolla narrow necked and urn shaped
- Height 6-18"
- Found at 6000-10,000' in elevation

Trees found in Mount Rainier National Park:

Western White Pine
Whitebark Pine
Lodgepole Pine
Ponderosa Pine
Engelman Spruce
Sitka Spruce
Western Hemlock
Mountain Hemlock
Douglas Fir
Grand Fir
Pacific Silver Fir
Noble Fir
Subalpine Fir

Western Red Cedar
Alaska Yellow Cedar
Western Yew
Scouler Willow
Pacific Willow
Black Willow
Red Alder
Pacific Dogwood
Bigleaf Maple
Vine Maple
Douglas Maple
Wild Crabapple
Bittercherry

DOUGLAS FIR

(Pseudotsuga menziesii)

Field Marks:
* Chunky, cinnamon-brown bark
* Hairy cones with 3 point bracts between the scales

Notes:
* Found at 4500' and below
* Height 200-300"
* Native Americans used the wood for: firewood, shafts for harpoons and salmon spears and the bark was boiled to produce a light brown dye.

(Abies lasiocarpa)

Field Marks:
- Needles blue to silvery green, flat and broad
- Cones grow upright on the upper branches.
- Cones are purplish-gray, flat topped and 2-4" long.
- Lower branches take root where they touch the ground.

Notes:
- Grows above 3000'
- Height 80-100'

ALASKA YELLOW CEDAR

(Chamaecyparis nootkatensis)

Field Marks:
* Ash-green bark
* Drooping leaves (yellow-green)
* Cones small and globe-like
* Young trees twisted grotesquely by snowpack

Notes:
* Found 3000-5000' in elevation
* Height 80-120'

(Thuja plicata)

Field Marks:
* Overlapping, fern-like branches
* Leaves a shiny dark yellow-green
* Dark reddish-brown bark (shredding)
* Cones small, ½ - ¾" long

Notes:
* A lower forest tree
* Has a shallow root system
* Native Americans use the wood for totem poles, lodges, canoes and cooking planks. They used the shredding bark for weaving mats and clothing.

MOUNTAIN HEMLOCK

(Tsuga mertensiana)

Field Marks:
* Dark green branches that lift upwards near their ends
* Cones 1½ - 3" long
* Young cones may appear purple.
* Leader tip droops.

Notes:
* Found between subalpine and timberline

(Tsuga heterophylla)

Field Marks:
* Scaly, dark reddish brown bark
* Irregular size needles ¼ - 1" long
* Needles dark green, flat, blunt at tip
* Cones ¾ - 1" long and grow at the tip of the branches
* Leader tip droops.

Notes:
* Found at 5000' and below
* Height 200'
* Takes 25-30 years before the tree will begin to produce seed

VOCABULARY

Adaptation: a special characteristic a plant or animal has to help it survive better

Alpine: above 7000 feet in elevation

Anthocyanin: a chemical pigment in plants which filters UV light and warms the plant

Carnivore: an animal that eats meat

Carrion: a dead animal

Diurnal: animals which are active in the daylight

Field Mark: an identifying feature on a plant or animal which is easily seen

Heliotropic: a plant which follows the path of the sun

Herbivore: an animal which eats plants

Hibernation: a true hibernator is an animal which sleeps during the winter when its body temperature and metabolic rate slow down

Inflorescence: a flower cluster on one stem

Nocturnal: animals which are active at night

Omnivore: an animal which eats both plants and meat

Pubescence: plant hair

Saprophyte: a plant which feeds on dead or decaying organic matter

Terrestrial: land dweller

Cascade & Olympic Natural History
by Daniel Mathews, 1988

A Field Guide to the Cascades & Olympics
by Stephen R. Whitney, 1983

Fieldbook of Natural History
by Palmer & Fowler, 1975

The History and Folklore of North American Wildflowers
by Timothy Coffey 1993

The Living Earth Book of North American Trees
by Gerald Jonas, 1993

Wildflowers of the Pacific Northwest
by Lewis J. Clark, 1976

The Natural History of Puget Sound Country
by Arthur R. Kruckeberg, 1995

Hardy Heather Species
by D. Metheny, 1991

Flora of the Pacific Northwest
by Leo Hitchcock & Arthur Cronquist, 1973

Trees and Shrubs for Pacific Northwest Gardens
by John & Carol Grant, 1990

Flora of Mount Rainier National Park
by C. Frank Brockman, 1947

The Textbook of Dendrology
by William Harlow & Ellwood Harrar, 1937

INDEX OF COMMON NAMES

INDEX OF SCIENTIFIC NAMES

ABOUT THE ARTISTS

Laura Fisher Romanelli lives in the Northwest drawing her creative inspirations from the natural world. She worked as a Ranger Naturalist for eleven years in the National Park Service and spent eight of those years at Paradise in Mount Rainier National Park. Observing and studying wildflowers is one of her greatest passions. Currently she owns and operates an art business, "Art of the Earth", producing natural history T-shirts and illustrations. You may contact her at:

"Art of the Earth",
P.O. Box 1117
Duvall, WA 98019

Sandy Harley calls northern Minnesota home. It is there that she is able to observe, often at close hand, the wildlife that she draws. For a number of years, she worked as a naturalist at Long Lake Conservation Center near Palisade. A self-taught artist, she works out of her home and sells her limited edition prints. In addition, she does wildlife and pet commissions. Her prints are also available in several northern Minnesota galleries. You may contact her at:

"Wilderness Wind"
20655 493rd Lane
McGregor, MN 55760

Dave Larson graduated from Huxley College in 1991 with a degree in environmental science and went on to work for the Peace Corps in Forestry. In 1994, Dave became a Natural Resource Manger for Mount Rainier National Park and most recently for Lava Beds National Monument in California. During his time with the Park Service, he became involved with ornithology. His projects have included the surveying of threatened owls, bird banding and breeding surveys. Drawing is a good way to pass time and give something back to the birds he observed.

Susan Picatti is a native Washingtonian. She lived in Washington's Cascade mountains for two years working at a ski area and planting trees. She has worked as a free-lance graphic designer for over twenty years and although most of her work is in political advertising, she has recently moved into book design. This is her first field guide. You may contact her at:
spicatti@drizzle.com

Joe Dreimiller is a former National Park Service ranger from Mount Rainier National Park. He has always enjoyed exploring the natural wonders of North America. Joe has worked throughout the United States as an outdoor educator/wilderness trip leader teaching natural history lessons. He came to Mount Rainier in 1988 and spent several seasons at Paradise. He has worked as a Meadow Restoration Ranger, Paradise Meadow Resource Management Ranger, Climbing Ranger and a Law Enforcement Ranger. He has also worked as a ranger at North Cascades National Park, Blake Island State Park and Everett City Parks. Currently, he is working as a Watershed Patrol Officer for the City of Everett. This book has been his dream for many years. He has wanted to create a simple pocket sized book to be used by all ages for easy identification of the plants and animals at Mount Rainier National Park and the Cascades.

Earthwindows.com

Come Open Your Eyes and Experience Nature

- Field Guide, Note cards, Glass etchings
- Lodging
- Weather and trail conditions
- Climbing information and Guide Services
- General Information on Mount Rainier